DR. THASHNA WALSH

7 Essential Life Skills all 13-15 year olds need to know now

Follow these lessons in your teens and be healthier, happier and have more time and money throughout your life.

Copyright © 2022 by Dr. Thashna Walsh

All rights reserved. No part of this publication may be reproduced, stored or transmitted in any form or by any means, electronic, mechanical, photocopying, recording, scanning, or otherwise without written permission from the publisher. It is illegal to copy this book, post it to a website, or distribute it by any other means without permission.

Dr. Thashna Walsh asserts the moral right to be identified as the author of this work.

Dr. Thashna Walsh has no responsibility for the persistence or accuracy of URLs for external or third-party Internet Websites referred to in this publication and does not guarantee that any content on such Websites is, or will remain, accurate or appropriate.

Designations used by companies to distinguish their products are often claimed as trademarks. All brand names and product names used in this book and on its cover are trade names, service marks, trademarks and registered trademarks of their respective owners. The publishers and the book are not associated with any product or vendor mentioned in this book. None of the companies referenced within the book have endorsed the book.

First edition

This book was professionally typeset on Reedsy.
Find out more at reedsy.com

Contents

1	Welcome and Introduction	1
2	Secret to Happiness (+1 Bonus Tip)	3
3	Be a Life Saver (+1 Bonus Tip)	9
4	Eat just one thing (+5 Bonus Tips)	12
5	Become a Time Lord (+3 Bonus Tips)	16
6	7 to 8 hours that will change your life (+1 Bonus Tip)	19
7	9 minutes is all you need (+1 Bonus Tip)	22
8	The future is bright (+1 Bonus Tip)	24
9	Reviews	28
10	Conclusions	30
11	Resources	32
	About the Author	35

1

Welcome and Introduction

Stressed out with exams? Feel like your life isn't as exciting as everyone else's on social media? Feel like adults don't listen to you? Struggle to fit in? Worried about your body image and looks? Friends and social life stressing you out? Feel like there's not enough time in the day? Don't know what to do in the future? Did the lockdown during Covid rock your self-confidence and leave you feeling like you've missed 2 years of your life?

The list goes on. It's surprising you're still a functioning human being with all these things happening at once. Well, don't worry, this book has your back.

Contained in the following pages is years of research all squeezed down into bitesize chunks of information, so you just get the juicy need-to-know facts without all the waffle. Each chapter will introduce each of the 7 essential life skills or life lessons to allow you to start applying them to your life straight away. Each chapter also has at least one juicy bonus tip to get even more out of your life.

If you do apply them, you will feel less stressed, healthier, have more time and most importantly feel better about yourself – not only now but in many years to come.

Welcome to a new perspective. I'm Dr Thashna Walsh and have spent years helping people with their physical health (as a Chiropractor) and their mental health (as a therapist). I've treated many teenagers in that time and not too long ago my daughter was in her teens and this got me thinking about what I've advised and taught all them through the years and how I could reach even more teenagers with these essential life skills? What better way to get the message to an even wider audience than writing this book. I wish I had known these things when I was your age and I truly believe, if you take all this book has to offer to heart, you will get a real kick start in life. Anyway, enough about me, this book is all about you so let's jump right in.

Oh, almost forgot, a massive thanks for buying the book. I'm truly grateful for your interest and I'm sure you will find some, if not all, of the content useful to change your life for the better.

2

Secret to Happiness (+1 Bonus Tip)

Do you spend most of your day comparing yourself to other people? Are you constantly worried about everything from not doing well in exams, to not fitting in with your friends or not looking a certain way? Are there so many random and unhelpful thoughts constantly whirring around in your mind that you just don't know what to think? If the answer is yes to any or all of these, or you could list many more things then don't worry, you are probably like every one of your closest friends and possibly everyone in your school.

So, if everyone is going about their lives in this way, then don't you think that it is a crazy way to live? If you don't think so then stop reading here, close the book and continue with your [insert descriptive word similar to crazy] life. It was nice briefly knowing you. Cheers. YOLO. Bye.

Still reading? That must mean you aren't crazy. Phew. Ok, let's continue.

The most important thing to say at this point is Don't Worry. You made the right decision to buy this book and to learn some super essential life skills or life lessons that probably every human being on the planet learns at some point and in one way or another. The cool thing is you are learning these at a young age and therefore you won't have to struggle through life and learn these things the hard way many years from now. You're already getting ahead in the game of life. Award yourself a gold medal.

So - what is the secret to happiness? – we'll get on to that very shortly, but first you need to me made aware of a truly magnificent, awesome, lit and amazing super power you already have inside you that can help you through the journey of life – YOUR BRAIN!

WHAAAAAAT! I hear you scream. My brain? Get real. I'm going back to the world of the crazy people above, see ya.

Still reading? Wow, there must be something truly special about you. I think you are starting to become the sort of person I like to hang around with. So what did I mean about your brain and super powers and all that? Ok let me explain.

YOU have the power right now to think differently. YOU have the power right now to do things differently. YOU have the power right now to react to things differently. YOU have the power right now to change the language your internal voice speaks to you with.

Let me give you an example – For a large part of my life I used to tell myself I hated going shopping for food. In my head I used to think the following - You have to get in the car (you'll soon be driving in no time at all by the way!), drive to the supermarket, load a trolley with food, unload the trolley onto the belt at the cash register, load the trolley back up with the food you've just unloaded into bag, load the bags into the car, drive back home, unload the bags of food and load all the unloaded (again) food into your cupboards. So much loading, unloading, loading, unloading.

However, now I approach life in a totally different way and the exact same experience I just described above can be described as follows – how blessed am I to own a car that can transport me in comfort and luxury to a palace of food, stuffed with foods from all over the world that I can pick and choose at my leisure, so I can cook some amazingly nutritious meals when I get back home. This is now how I think about going food shopping.

Which of the above descriptions sounds the most fun and exciting? Hopefully you'll agree with me that a 'palace of food from all over the world' is the winner. By changing how I think about the experience has a knock-on effect to how my mind and body reacts to that thought. Instead of getting all grumpy, frustrated and agitated I now feel calm, relaxed and excited to see all these amazing foods from around the world.

Our thoughts affect us physically (Resource Ref 1 - click here). Different chemicals are released within our bodies depending on if we're feeling stressed or anxious (bad natural chemicals) or feeling happy and excited (good natural chemicals). Don't believe me?

Try this – stand up and then stand how you would stand if you were feeling unhappy and sad. I bet you dropped your shoulders, slouched and looked down. When stood like this notice how you feel. Do you feel like you don't have much energy?

Now stand up and stand how you would stand if you were feeling amazing and really excited. Are you standing the opposite to the way you were just standing? Is your head held high, shoulders back and maybe your are smiling? If not smile and then notice how you feel. Do you feel like you have a lot more energy and feel more alive? Ideally, this is how you want to approach life – full of positive energy, smiling and confident.

So, would you rather have good or bad natural chemicals swimming around your body? Of course you want the good stuff because your mental (and physical) health are improved. So, to get the good stuff means you need to feel happy more. Ah! Bingo. Happiness, we're back on to that subject, but what is the secret to achieving this?

THE SECRET IS: GRATITUDE
   (Resource Ref 2 - Blueprint for Happiness - https://www.tonyrobbins.com/mind-meaning/a-new-blueprint-for-happiness/)

Huh! You made me read all that to learn that. Trust me. It truly is the secret to living a happier life. If you go through life feeling grateful all the time you will never feel any bad stress, anger or frustration and your mental and physical health will be, well, healthier for it.

So how do I go about feeling grateful I hear you ask. Well, you have to train your brain from its current way of thinking to a more positive way of thinking.

STEP 1 - Start by learning some better words you can use when thinking about situations, such as:

Grateful, amazing, fun, awesome, blessed, magical, outstanding, happy, fulfilling, grateful (again!), generous, love, calm, peaceful, free, delightful, exceptional, beautiful, super, excellent, fabulous, spectacular, best, lovely.... etc

Write in a notepad some positive words that you normally use.

STEP 2 – Whenever you don't feel good about something or have negative thoughts try and become aware of yourself feeling or thinking this way and immediately think differently.

For example – if you stuck in a traffic jam and feel bored and frustrated ask yourself the following question "Can I change the situation?". The answer is probably no, then ask yourself "Can I change how I think and react to this situation?". The answer to this question is always yes. So, you can change how you react and start thinking more positive thoughts.

Also, look for ways to positively take advantage of the situation. In the example above you could use this as an opportunity to talk to your mum/dad about something or to get a head start on some homework if you're coming back from school.

STEP 3 – Before going to sleep at night write at least one thing (but the more the better) you were grateful for that day.

Keep repeating the above steps for at least 1 month and you should notice yourself starting to think differently and start to feel happier.

STEP 4 - Even better, talk to your mum, dad, brothers, sisters or whoever makes up your family unit and get them involved. If you see one of them feeling a bit grumpy you can remind them of the above steps and to change their thoughts and they can remind you if you feel grumpy and don't become aware of it before they do.

Repeating the above steps until they form into a habit is the key, i.e. these steps become something that you naturally do without even thinking about it. Once you've created a new habit you'll find you just think differently for every situation you come across.

Give it a go. You have the super power! Use your powers for good.

BONUS TIP 1 – give more and keep learning/growing. Give more of your attention to friends. Give more of your time to helping your mum/dad around the house. Give thoughtful presents to the people you love. The act of giving and making someone else's day will bring you joy and happiness. If you keep learning throughout your life you will also keep growing (mentally) and this will fulfil your life and make you feel happier in the long run.

3

Be a Life Saver (+1 Bonus Tip)

Be a life saver? What like a lifeguard or something? Well, you could do this, as having a job that potentially saves someone else's life is a great thing. Actually, what I mean is save money over the course of your life.

Ok, you might not have any money at the moment, but maybe you get some pocket money or have a job like delivering newspapers, washing cars, walking dogs, babysitting, social media influencer, whatever. The point is to get in the habit of saving and the SOONER YOU GET INTO THE SAVING HABIT all the better for you in years to come.

Have you ever heard of the magical power of compound interest? No? Let me explain.

Imagine you could save $10 or £10 (whatever currency, let's assume $) per month and you put this in a bank paying 2% interest per year and you paid no tax. The approximate amounts you would have after a number of years are below:
   1 year = $121
   5 years = $631

10 years = $1329
20 years = $2952
30 years = $4935
40 years = $7356
50 years = $10313

The amount keeps getting higher and higher the longer you leave it. If you can save the money as soon as you get it and put it straight into an account that you never ever touch this removes any temptation to spend it.

The point of earning money though is mainly to pay to live somewhere, eat, enjoy life and to help those less well off (remember the Bonus tip from the last section), therefore a good rule of thumb is to save 10% of everything that you earn from now on and put it into the long term DON'T TOUCH pot. So get in the habit of saving some of what you earn and put it somewhere you can't easily access and let the magic of compound interest work in your favour.

THE MORE MONEY YOU SAVE EACH MONTH AND THE LONGER THE TIME YOU SAVE IT OVER, THE BIGGER THE POT OF MONEY AT THE END.

You may have to switch saving accounts at times so you keep getting the best interest rate (the higher the interest rate the bigger the magic). If you haven't got a bank/savings account ask your mum/dad/responsible adult to set you one up.

When you finally start to work for a living, you'll be earning and saving a lot more than $10 a month and if you get into this saving habit for life you will reap the rewards when you are older.

BONUS TIP 1 – credit cards (which you won't be able to get until you are older) seem like they offer easy money. Get in the habit of earning/saving for something you want rather than using easily available credit to buy something. It is very easy to get into debt with credit cards so avoid them AT ALL COSTS.

4

Eat just one thing (+5 Bonus Tips)

Ok, here we go again. Eat just one thing? What, like live off bananas for the rest of my life? Ermm, not quite. What I mean by this is eat real food with just one ingredient, i.e. a banana, an apple, broccoli, cabbage, carrot etc.

There is a lot of food around that is highly processed, full of the wrong kind of fats and loaded with sugar and salt. Have a look at the stuff in your cupboards and check out the ingredients label. As soon as you're getting above 5 ingredients and those ingredients sound like something that should be used to clean ovens (rather than eaten) then it is a good bet that it is processed.

There's a ton of stuff about diets and nutrition in books and on the internet, but keep it simple. Eat real food that has one ingredient, i.e. itself.

The more green stuff you can eat the better, but also eat different coloured foods such as red peppers, white cauliflower, orange carrots etc. All those different colours mean lots of different nutrients and your health should improve as a result. See "The 12 Steps of Pure Energy" guide here:

Tony Robbins - The 12 steps of pure energy
  (Resource Ref 3)

EAT THESE FOODS:

1. Eat lots of green foods because they are alkaline and protect your body from disease
2. Eat the rainbow or multicoloured foods to get an abundance of different nutrients
3. Drink lots of water, preferably with lemon squeezed in to alkalise your body
4. Eat nuts – they are packed with vitamins, minerals, protein and good fats (not salted peanuts)
5. Eat pulses like beans, lentils and peas – they are high in protein and fibre and low in fat

AVOID THESE FOODS:

1. Processed food full of lots of unreadable ingredients – they are full of saturated fats and salt
2. Fizzy drinks – they are loaded with sugar and will cause you to put on weight whilst rotting your teeth at the same time
3. Dairy such as milk and cheese – they are full of saturated fats and are very acidic
4. Meat – it is full of saturated fat and farming practices aren't generally kind to the planet
5. Coffee – one cup may be ok but many people drink far too much during the day, which can lead to health issues such as hypertension

and lack of sleep (insomnia)

BONUS TIP 1 - Worried about climate change? (Resource Ref 4 - click here)

If so, you can take the decision right now to become vegan. A vegan is someone who doesn't eat meat or dairy (like Milk and cheese) and studies have shown it is the best diet in respect of taking care of the planet and your carbon footprint. Hopefully you have learned all about climate change at school. If not, discuss it with your mum/dad/responsible adult. Try and eat food which has been grown locally, which is even better for the climate, since local food has fewer delivery miles linked to it.

BONUS TIP 2 – Drink lots of water. Avoid fizzy drinks which are loaded with sugar and will rot your teeth.

BONUS TIP 3 – Whilst we're on the subject of teeth. Look after them as no new teeth will grow now. Brush at least twice a day, floss and use mouthwash. Do all this whilst eating less sugar and you'll have lovely teeth into old age.

BONUS (future) TIP 4 – Alcohol. If alcohol was just discovered now, it would probably be classed similarly to a class A drug. Alcohol is expensive and you are effectively paying to put poison inside your body. My advice is to develop a strong, happy and confident mindset and save what money you may have spent poisoning yourself and add it to your long-term savings pot.

BONUS (future) TIP 5 – Smoking. Don't do it. It isn't cool. It will kill you and you will spend a lot of money in the pursuit of your early death.

EAT JUST ONE THING (+5 BONUS TIPS)

Do you really want to drink this:

[QR code]

15

5

Become a Time Lord (+3 Bonus Tips)

Are you feeling like your life isn't as exciting as everyone else's on social media or your body isn't as nice? Do you feel like there's not enough time in the day to do chores, schoolwork and see friends?

The solution to all of these is SIGN OUT of social media. Log off. Quit.

How long do you spend per day on social media? Whatever it is, that is the amount of time you'll get back per day to do better things, simply by signing out. If you have never watched "The Social Dilemma" on Netflix (Resource Ref 5 - The Social Dilemma - https://www.thesocialdilemma.com/) I recommend you watching it. The most telling part of that film for me was the interviews with the software designers who were asked the question "would you let your children use social media?". All of them said no.

Just look at the dilemmas listed below the movie. The 2016 presidential election between Donald Trump and Hilary Clinton was heavily influenced by social media: click here (Resource Ref 6)

Lots of fake social media accounts touting conspiracy theories and other fake news. It is difficult to know what is true and what isn't these days, so do yourself a favour and don't just believe something you read or see just because it looks fancy or your friends believe it. Use common sense and research around a subject if you are unsure.

Scary stuff! It is like mind control!

Social media is purposefully designed to constantly grab your attention 24 hours a day. Studies (Resource Ref 7 - click here) have shown it is as addictive as drugs and alcohol and we all know how bad they are for you.

Don't get me wrong, social media is a great way to stay in touch with people, especially if they don't live near you, but if you mainly have negative thoughts when using social media or find yourself constantly thinking if someone has liked your recent post - do yourself a massive favour and sign out. Most people who post a lot on social media, showing everyone else how great their life is, are doing so from a deep-rooted need for recognition. In other words, they are doing it from a negative place. Don't let their neediness affect your life in a negative way.

The secret to staying mentally healthy online is:

YOU CONTROL WHEN YOU LOOK AT SOCIAL MEDIA RATHER THAN SOCIAL MEDIA CONTROLLING YOU!

Say you used social media for about 2 hours a day on average. Try limiting your use to only 15mins per day (never at bedtime) and use the extra 1 hour and 45 mins (or whatever the number is) you have just instantly gained to spend more time actually face to face with your friends or you could have more time to get your schoolwork done rather than feeling stressed about it. You could start a new hobby (remember the BONUS TIP 1 in chapter 1?) or do exercise, which will help you stay fit and healthy and reduce any feelings of stress. Signing out of social media and doing exercise is a double stress busting win!

When you are online, please follow these BONUS TIPS:

BONUS TIP 1 – Stay safe online. Never post pictures of yourself online or send pictures to someone on your phone. Think of it as the same as printing off 1000's copies of that picture and then posting each of those copies through the letterboxes of all the houses in your neighbourhood. Would you post that picture through your neighbour's letterbox? If not, don't do it online or on your phone. Also remember, the internet is global and not just your neighbourhood, so any pictures could end up online anywhere and everywhere and stay there for a very long time.

BONUS TIP 2 – Stay safe online. Beware of chatting to someone online that you don't know. Or, if the profile picture is someone you know, but the conversation feels wrong then it could be a complete stranger you are in a conversation with. That stranger could be a 50 year old man/woman anywhere in the world. Think about that the next time you are in an online conversation and whether you would be comfortable saying what you are about to say to a 50 year old male/female stranger.

BONUS TIP 3 – Be kind online. Think about being online as being face to face with someone. Would you say a nasty thing directly to someone's face? If not, don't say it online. Remember the positive stuff you learned in chapter 1 and don't spread hate. If you have been practising the positive and grateful mindset AND you have signed out of social media you really won't feel any need to spend hours online writing negative things about people. Hopefully you never did this anyway.

6

7 to 8 hours that will change your life (+1 Bonus Tip)

Sleep is very very important for life. If you don't believe me read the following: Click Here (Resource Ref 8)

As the article says, your body naturally heals itself during sleep and if you don't get enough sleep you'll feel grumpy with no energy for life. Lack of sleep has also been linked to brain degenerative diseases such as Alzheimer's

A new Stanford University study finds lack of sleep linked to Alzheimer's disease. Watch a quick video here (Resource Ref 9) :

(Just select camera on your phone, select photo and then look at this QR code through your phone – a link should pop up to take you to a quick news story video)

How much sleep do you currently get? Are you getting 7-8 hours?

Do you find it hard to sleep because your mind is constantly thinking or you are constantly worried about things? Practicing what was taught in chapter 1 will help, exercising will help, not using your phone/tablet/laptop in bed will help.

Bedtime routines may sound boring, but they work. We all have our natural body clocks – some people function better in the morning, whilst others may struggle to get out of bed early and function better in the evening, when the morning people are starting to get sleepy. Listen to your body and try and figure out what your natural body clock is.

To figure out what your natural body clock is, try the following on a weekend or on a night when you don't have to get up for anything the next day – in the evening make a note of the time you start to feel sleepy and then go to bed. Don't set an alarm as your aim is to try and wake up naturally. When you wake up the next day (hopefully naturally and not because the dog barked or your parents shouted at you), make a note of the time. Just double check that you are happy that you fell asleep naturally and you woke up naturally. If so, those times should give you a decent idea what your natural body clock is. Is it within the ideal time of 7-8 hours?

Hopefully you don't have trouble falling asleep and you naturally got 7-8 hours. If not, keep reading.

Once you know your natural body clock times, set a sleep routine around these times. A typical time to sleep is between 10pm to 6am, but whatever your times are make sure they allow you to get to school on time.

A good sleep routine is as follows:

1. Go to bed and wake up at the same time (ideally your natural body clock times) each day
2. Ensure you haven't eaten anything about 3-4 hours before your natural sleep time
3. Ensure your bedroom is as dark as possible and on the cool side. Maybe you can leave a window open to get some cool overnight fresh air into your bedroom, but only if you live in a quietish neighbourhood.
4. DON'T use your phone, tablet or laptop before bed and especially when in your bedroom. You need to create a habit whereby your brain knows it is now sleep time.
5. Exercise helps with sleep, as do the steps outlined in chapter one
6. DON'T wake up and immediately look at your devices. The morning is the perfect time to do some exercise (see next chapter). Exercise will get you physically healthier and will also help you with your sleep. Sleep also helps with your physical and mental health. As you can see it is a circular win win.

BONUS TIP 1 – Meditation and deep breathing help to calm the mind. There are plenty of meditation and breathing apps available. Talk with your mum/dad/responsible adult to get their help picking a suitable app for you to try. Preferably practise using the app during the day, and once you know what to do, try the meditation/breathing just before bed so your mind can start to wind down and feel relaxed. Remember - you should have already switched off your devices by now anyway .

7

9 minutes is all you need (+1 Bonus Tip)

Did you know you only need to do three 3 minute high intensity blasts of exercise per week to see some real health benefits such as improving your heart health? Yep, you heard me, only 3 minutes three times a week (click here - Resource Ref 10).

Here's how you do it. Do exercises on alternate days and rest on the days in between. The trick to the exercises is to do them so intensely and for the full 3 minutes, so by the end of the 3 minutes your heart is pounding and you are breathing really heavily.

Some exercises you can do involve no equipment and can be done anywhere, these include:

- Star jumps
- Running on the spot with high knees
- Squatting and jumping
- Mountain climbers

If you are unsure what these exercises are then do a quick internet search. They're simple and almost anyone can do them. If you have difficulty doing exercises or are in a wheelchair for example then any fast, repetitive movements using as much of your body as possible should do the trick. Always double check with your mum/dad/responsible adult that it is ok for you to do exercises, especially if you have any underlying health conditions. Or if you are really unsure then double check with your doctor.

So here is what a typical exercise week may look like:
   Monday – 3 minutes of star jumps
   Tuesday – rest day
   Wednesday – 3 minutes of running on the spot
   Thursday – rest day
   Friday – 3 minutes of squat jumps
   Saturday – rest day
   Sunday – rest day

And that is it. If you do the exercises as described above you should see some health benefits. Remember, as we discussed in the last chapter, exercising should also help you sleep and having good quality sleep is also good for your health.

BONUS TIP 1 – do some swimming and/or brisk walking which are also great for your health. You may have heard of people trying to do 10,000 steps a day to lose weight and keep fit. 10,000 steps are approximately 5 miles and unfortunately it can take well over an hour to walk five miles. Brisk or fast walking for 10 minutes is just as good, if not better for you to improve your health.

8

The future is bright (+1 Bonus Tip)

Ok, we're nearly at the end. I know, it's gone so quick, but I've enjoyed your company so far and hopefully you'll stick around until the end. This chapter is all about thinking about what you are going to do in the future. Maybe you already know what you want to do, maybe you have thought about it but have no clue or maybe you haven't even thought about it. Whichever one of these situations best describes you doesn't really matter. The main thing is actively thinking about it and actively trying different things to discover what you like or don't like.

The most important thing to consider is not what the job specifically is and how much money it pays, but how the job makes you feel. In other words DO SOMETHING YOU LOVE. The most fulfilling jobs are usually those that help other people or animals and/or contribute positively to society and the world.

Try the following simple steps:

STEP 1 – write a list of at least 10 things you love doing and WHY you love doing them. It doesn't matter if you think other people will think they are boring, if you enjoy doing it that is the important thing. Now see if you can answer yes to any or all of the following questions for each of the things in your list. Start with the first thing your wrote down and answer the following:

1. Can you do this thing well and effortlessly?
2. Do you lose track of time when you do this thing because you are enjoying it so much?
3. Do you naturally want to learn more about this thing and get better at it?
4. Have you been interested in this thing for a long time?
5. Do your friends and family often mention how much you like this thing when they talk about you?
6. When you encounter a problem doing this thing, you are eager to try and solve it rather than just give up.

STEP 2 – write a list of at least 10 things you hate doing and WHY you hate doing them.

STEP 3 – ask your friends and parents to describe your strengths or what they think you are good at.

STEP 4 – Describe your perfect day. What is it like and what do you do?

STEP 5 – Look at all the things you have written in steps 1, 3 and 4 and pick out the most common themes in each of these steps.

Is a clearer picture starting to emerge? Don't worry if there isn't as you still have a lot of time on your side. A great way of finding what you love or hate doing is by actually trying it. Make a conscious effort over the next few years to try lots of different things such as:

- Try a new hobby
- Join a new group
- Try a new sport
- Read new books about different subjects
- Talk to your parents, grandparents and friends' parents and ask them what jobs they do, what the job involves, what skills are needed for the job and why they enjoy (or hate) the job.

And don't worry about failing at something: "THE ONLY TRUE FAILURE IS THE FAILURE TO TRY"

BONUS TIP 1 - It is also a good idea to try and think what the world will be like in the future and what 'new' jobs people might be doing that maybe don't even exist yet. How about some of these for ideas: click here (Resource Ref 11). Here's just a few from the list:

1. *Organ Creator* – crating organs from stem cells. Key subjects to study in this area include molecular biology, tissue engineering, or biomedical engineering.
2. *Augmented-reality journey builder* – have you seen the film "Ready Player One" (Resource Ref 12 - https://www.imdb.com/title/tt1677720/)? If not, check it out, it is a great film. Anyway, you could be building these virtual worlds. Key subjects to study in this area include film and cinematography, massive multiplayer online role-playing game development.
3. *Makeshift structure engineer* – with climate change likely to cause more natural disasters around the world a makeshift structure engineer will use their skills to 3D print structures quickly for use in disaster zones. Key subjects to study in this area include industrial design and structural engineering.
4. *Rewilder* – someone who turns disused factories and buildings into

bio-diverse green belts. Key subjects to study in this area include agriculture, wildlife management, and environmental science.
5. *Drone traffic optimizer* – if companies like Amazon get their way there will be automated drones flying around everywhere delivering parcels and pizzas and, who knows, maybe even people in the future. Someone will need to oversee all these flight paths. Or maybe you could be the computer programmer that develops the algorithms to stop all the drones and self-driving cars from crashing into each other.
6. *Autonomous Car Mechanic* – combine old school mechanic skills with cutting edge autonomous vehicle skills to fix all those cars of the future.

I'll let you read the rest. Just search for "jobs of the future" and see what pops up. Maybe something will catch your eye and spark an interest. If it does, think about why it interests you, because your body's reaction to things is usually a signal to the brain that something either feels right or feels wrong. Listen to these signals and never ignore them.

9

Reviews

If you enjoyed this book and found the information useful it would mean the world to me if you could leave a good review. You will be helping other teens get a head start in life if you leave a review because the more reviews the book gets, the more likely other teens will come across the book and therefore be able to make use of the information. Think of this as you doing your 'Giving' part as described in the bonus tip in chapter one.

If you require more help with your own issues I would love to hear from you. You can book a FREE no obligation Zoom call with me to discuss any issues you may be struggling with and to determine whether we're a good fit for working together to solve your problems.

BOOK A FREE NO OBLIGATION DISCOVERY CALL HERE:

https://654388.17hats.com/p#/scheduling/szgcvzsdtwrfxdzwtxzcvpkswhzxrrhn

Or visit my website to read more about how I can help here:
www.thashnawalsh.com

You can also find more information in my blogs here:
www.thashnawalsh.com/blog

For more meditations go here:
www.thashnawalsh.com/twlt-meditations

10

Conclusions

Wow, that went quick, but well done you on sticking to the end. If you have just learned one thing whilst reading this book that will make me happy. If you have learned lots then that will make me even more happy.

If you apply everything you have learned in this book, and consistently keep applying what you have learned until it becomes just what you do (i.e. a habit), then in about 6 month's to a year's time, here is what your life might look like:

You've signed out of social media or dramatically limited your usage of it and this has freed up more time to learn new things and try new hobbies. You are sleeping much better, doing exercise and eating healthier and therefore have more energy and zest for life. You now see the world from a grateful perspective and therefore never feel any stress or anxiety and walk around with a constant smile on your face because you are happy. You have a part time job and are now always saving some money so you will have lots to spend in the future when you are older. You really like the look of a future job and have decided to find out more about it and this is now affecting your decisions on what subjects to study at school.

Let's try and sum that up in as few words as possible:

You are a HAPPY, HEALTHY, LEARNING, GROWING, RICHER and FOCUSSED teen wizard!

Go forth into the world and cast your amazing spells for the good of humanity.

Have an outstanding life!

11

Resources

RESOURCES

1. Smalley, S. (2011, May 25). Mind Body Medicine: Can What You Think and Feel Affect Your Physical Health? Huff Post. Retrieved May 29, 2022, from https://www.huffpost.com/entry/how-whats-in-your-mind-ef_b_772813

2. Team Tony. (n.d.). A NEW BLUEPRINT FOR HAPPINESS. Tony Robbins. Retrieved May 29, 2022, from https://www.tonyrobbins.com/mind-meaning/a-new-blueprint-for-happiness/

3. Team Tony. (n.d.-b). THE 10-DAY HEALTH CHALLENGE. Tony Robbins. Retrieved May 29, 2022, from https://www.tonyrobbins.com/health-vitality/the-10-day-pure-energy-challenge/

4. Henriques, M. (2022, May 2). The climate benefits of veganism and vegetarianism. BBC. Retrieved May 29, 2022, from https://www.bbc.com/future/article/20220429-the-climate-benefits-of-veganism-and-vegetarianism

5. The Social Dilemma. (n.d.). The Social Dilemma. Retrieved May 29, 2022, from https://www.thesocialdilemma.com/

6. Social media in the 2016 United States presidential election. (2022, May 27). Wikipedia. Retrieved May 29, 2022, from https://en.wikipedia.org/wiki/Social_media_in_the_2016_United_States_presidential_election

7. Hilliard, J. (2019, September 4). New Study Suggests Excessive Social Media Use Is Comparable To Drug Addiction. Addiction Center. Retrieved May 29, 2022, from https://www.addictioncenter.com/news/2019/09/excessive-social-media-use/

8. American Sleep Association. (n.d.). Why is Sleep Important? Retrieved May 29, 2022, from https://www.sleepassociation.org/blog-post/why-is-sleep-important/

9. Good Morning America. (2021, September 1). New Stanford University study finds lack of sleep linked to Alzheimer's disease. Retrieved May 29, 2022, from https://youtu.be/xyprysmNO7A

10. Mosley, M. (n.d.). Fast exercise. Michael Mosley - Fast Exercise. Retrieved May 29, 2022, from https://www.fast-exercises.com/michael-answers-frequently-asked-questions/

11. Anderson, B. M. (2022, May 16). 15 Jobs You'll Be Recruiting for in 2030. Linkedin. Retrieved May 29, 2022, from https://www.linkedin.com/business/talent/blog/talent-strategy/jobs-you-will-be-recruiting-for-in-2030

12. Ready Player One. (n.d.). IMDb. Retrieved May 29, 2022, from https://www.imdb.com/title/tt1677720/

About the Author

As a Chiropractor and hypnotherapist I specialise in healing the body AND mind and I have treated numerous teenagers throughout my career. I'm also a mother to a beautiful daughter who was a teenager herself not so long ago. This book stemmed from the advice I was always giving to them on how to live better.

You can connect with me on:
- https://thashnawalsh.com
- https://www.facebook.com//TWLTing
- https://www.instagram.com/thashna_walsh_lifestyle

Printed in Great Britain
by Amazon